X-TREME FACTS: NATURAL DISASTERS

EARTHQUAKES

by Marcia Abramson

BEARPORT
PUBLISHING

Minneapolis, Minnesota

Credits:

© Title Page, 11 middle, US Air Force/Public Domain; 4 top, Public Domain; 4 bottom, jeremykingnz/Shutterstock; 5 top, COLOMBO NICOLA/Shutterstock.com; 5 middle, Alessia Pierdomenico/Shutterstock.com; 5 bottom, Jurik Peter/Shutterstock; 5 bottom left, 5 bottom right, Louella938/Shutterstock; 5 bottom middle, Design Projects/Shutterstock; 6, LukaKikina/Shutterstock; 6 bottom left, 6 bottom right, 1968/Shutterstock; 7 top, Pixel-Shot/Shutterstock; 7 top right, kimberrywood/Shutterstock; 7 middle, Schwede66/Creative Commons; 7 bottom, Fotos593/Shutterstock.com; 8 top, Kolonko/Shutterstock; 8 bottom, Naypong Studio/Shutterstock; 9 top, Amadeu Blasco/Shutterstock; 9 bottom, Olga Danylenko/Shutterstock; 9 left, everst/Shutterstock; 9 right, 10 botttom right, Anatoliy Karlyuk/Shutterstock; 10 top, Osaze Cuomo/Shutterstock; 10 bottom, OPIS Zagreb/Shutterstock.com; 10 bottom left, oman Samborskyi/Shutterstock; 11 top, Fotos593/Shutterstock.com; 11 top left, 26 bottom left, LightField Studios/Shutterstock; 11 bottom, Willyam Bradberry/Shutterstock; 11 bottom left, metha1819/Shutterstock; 12 bottom, Katoosha/Shutterstock; 12 bottom middle, matrioshka/Shutterstock; 13 top, gsrsirji/Shutterstock; 13 top right, NOAA/NGDC, G. Pflafker, U.S. Geological Survey/Public Domain; 13 middle, Apcbg/Creative Commons; 13 bottom, Guitar photographer/Shutterstock; 13 bottom center, NASA/Public Domain;/13 bottom left, 13 bottom right, Design Projects/Shutterstock; 14, Roberto Destarac Photo/Shutterstock; 14 bottom, USGS/Public Domain; 15 top, H.D. Chadwick/Public Domain;15 bottom, sanbeiji/Joe Lewi/Creative Commons; 15 bottom middle left, Marko Poplasen Marko Poplasen/Shutterstock; 15 bottom right, Gelpi/Shutterstock; 16 top, Ruthven/Creative Commons; 16 United States Geological Survey/Public Domain; 16 bottom right, Maridav/Shutterstock; 17 top, Fotos593/Shutterstock; 17 top left, fizkes/Shutterstock; 17 top middle, paffy/Shutterstock; 17 middle, astudio/Shutterstock; 17 bottom left, ArCaLu/Shutterstock; 17 bottom, ArCaLu/Shutterstock; 18, IgorZh/Shutterstock; 18 top right, Mass Communication Specialist 3rd Class Dylan McCord/United States Navy/Public Domain; 18 top, United States Navy/Public Domain;18 bottom, Susanna Loof/IAEA/Creative Commons; 19 top, David Rydevik/Public Domain; 19 middle right, U.S. Navy photo by Photographer's Mate 2nd Class Philip A. McDaniel/United States Navy/Public Domain; 19 middle, Alex Izeman/Shutterstock; 19 bottom, Edmund Lowe Photography/Shutterstock; 20 top, 20 bottom, Buonasera/Creative Commons; 21 top, Trevor Clark/Shutterstock; 21 top middle, Ruslana Iurchenko/Shutterstock; 21 top right, 21 bottom, NOAA/Public Domain; 22 top, John Masefield/Public Domain; 22 bottom, Puzzle studio/Shutterstock; 22 bottom left, Mamuka Gotsiridze/Shutterstock; 22 bottom right, artincamera/Shutterstock; 23 top, UN Photo/Logan Abassi United Nations Development Programme/Creative Commons; 23 top right, U.S. Navy photo by Mass Communication Specialist 2nd Class Kristopher Wilson/Public Domain; 23 bottom, US Department of Defense/Public Domain; 23 bottom left, Studio Romantic/Shutterstock; 23 bottom right, Pormezz/Shutterstock; 24 top, David Pereiras/Shutterstock; 24 bottom, New Africa/Shutterstock; 24 bottom middle, polkadot_photo/Shutterstock; 25 top, 4.murat/Shutterstock.com; 25 middle, David and Jessie Cowhig/Creative Commons; 25 bottom, Prometheus72/Shutterstock.com; 25 bottom left, andregric/Shutterstock; 25 bottom right, LiskaM/Shutterstock; 26 top, Armand du Plessis/Creative Commons; 26 middle, saiko3p/Shutterstock; 26 bottom right, Anne-Louis Girodet de Roussy-Trioson/Public Domain; 27 top, Georgios Tsichlis/Shutterstock; 27 top right, Jenny Sturm/Shutterstock; 27 middle, Paul Looyen/Shutterstock; 27 bottom, cb_travel/Shutterstock; 27 bottom left, Luis Molinero/Shutterstock; 27 bottom middle, mary981/Shutterstock; 27 bottom right, pathdoc/Shutterstock; 28 top left, VisualProduction/Shutterstock; 28 bottom left, Falconaumanni/Creative Commons; 28 top right, Irina Rogova/Shutterstock; 28 middle right, indigolotos/Shutterstock; 28 bottom right, Pressmaster/Shutterstock; 29, Austen Photography

Bearport Publishing Company Product Development Team

President: Jen Jenson; Director of Product Development: Spencer Brinker; Managing Editor: Allison Juda; Associate Editor: Naomi Reich; Associate Editor: Tiana Tran; Senior Designer: Colin O'Dea; Associate Designer: Elena Klinkner; Associate Designer: Kayla Eggert; Product Development Specialist: Anita Stasson

Produced for Bearport Publishing by BlueAppleWorks Inc.
Managing Editor for BlueAppleWorks: Melissa McClellan
Art Director: T.J. Choleva
Photo Research: Jane Reid

Library of Congress Cataloging-in-Publication Data is available at www.loc.gov or upon request from the publisher.

ISBN: 979-8-88509-977-6 (hardcover)
ISBN: 979-8-88822-157-0 (paperback)
ISBN: 979-8-88822-297-3 (ebook)

Copyright © 2024 Bearport Publishing Company. All rights reserved. No part of this publication may be reproduced in whole or in part, stored in any retrieval system, or transmitted in any form or by any means, electronic, mechanical, photocopying, recording, or otherwise, without written permission from the publisher.

For more information, write to Bearport Publishing, 5357 Penn Avenue South, Minneapolis, MN 55419.

Contents

On Shaky Ground 4

Earth Movers 6

Faulty Crust 8

Tipping the Scales 10

Ripple Effects 12

The Ring of Fire 14

Cracking Up 16

Walls of Water 18

A Monster Quake 20

Death and Destruction 22

Drop, Cover, and Hold! 24

Shaking but Not Breaking 26

Fruity Fissures 28

Glossary 30

Read More 31

Learn More Online 31

Index 32

About the Author 32

On Shaky Ground

It's a calm day until suddenly the ground begins shaking. Books tumble off shelves, and dishes shatter in cabinets. The walls are wiggling, and some buildings are even toppling to the ground. The rumbling seems to be making noise for miles, and there's no telling when it will stop. But in just half a minute, the shaking stops. The earthquake is finally over.

Japan has the most earthquakes of any country. An old folktale says they are caused by a giant catfish splashing around.

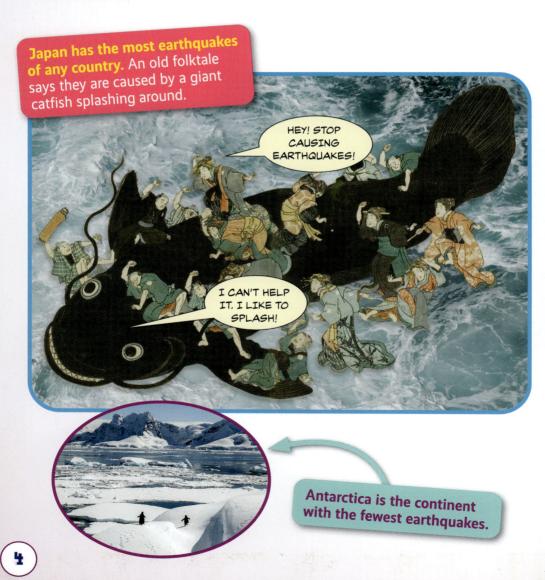

Antarctica is the continent with the fewest earthquakes.

Alaska experiences the most earthquakes in the United States. California's earthquakes cause the most damage.

Earth Movers

Earthquakes may seem like they can come out of nowhere. But there are actually some warning signs. That is, if you can feel very minor shifting under your feet. Many quakes are so small that they happen without us noticing. Some of these small shakes lead to bigger earthmoving moments. Other natural disasters can also cause an earthquake.

Earthquakes can strike at any time, in any season, and in any kind of weather.

IF THERE'S AN EARTHQUAKE, THEY WON'T BE ABLE TO BLAME THE MINERS.

LOOK AT THAT VOLCANO ERUPT!

Landslides and volcanic eruptions can cause earthquakes. And so can people! Some kinds of mining may lead to quakes.

Foreshocks are small earthquakes that come before a quake's big shock.

IT'S BEEN TWO MONTHS SINCE THE EARTHQUAKE HIT. WHAT'S GOING ON?

Powerful aftershocks can shake the ground days, months, or even years after an earthquake.

A 2011 aftershock in New Zealand was worse than the main earthquake!

Most earthquakes are too small to notice. You may have experienced an earthquake without even knowing it!

Only about 100 quakes each year are strong enough to cause damage.

Faulty Crust

Intense earthquakes leave visible signs aboveground. But much of the action happens due to Earth's layers below the surface. The crust is Earth's outer rocky layer. The mantle is the layer below that. It contains **tectonic** plates—giant **slabs** of rock. These plates move around slowly over Earth's superhot liquid-rock core. The places where the plates rub against one another and release their quaking energy are called faults. Most of the world's earthquakes happen along these fault lines.

The planet's largest tectonic plate **is under the Pacific Ocean.**

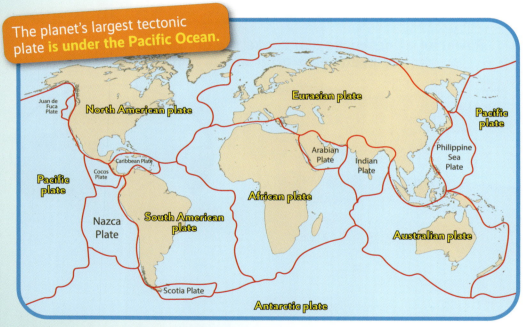

There are seven major tectonic plates. They are under the Pacific Ocean, North America, South America, Eurasia, Australia, Africa, and Antarctica.

A tectonic plate movement **of just inches can set off a major quake.**

The hypocenter is the exact spot underground where two plates get stuck against each other to cause an earthquake.

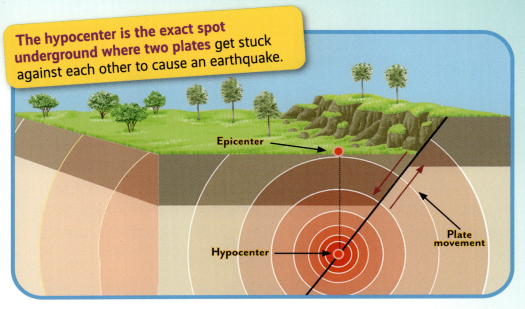

If you go straight up from the hypocenter to the surface, you're at a quake's epicenter. This is where the most powerful and destructive shaking happens.

Los Angeles, California, could end up next to San Francisco—a shift of 350 miles (560 km)—in millions of years thanks to the very active San Andreas Fault.

Deep ocean gashes open when one plate pushes another down. The Mariana Trench in the Pacific reaches a record depth of 7 miles (11 km)!

Mountains grow where plates collide, causing Earth's crust to push upward. The bigger the crunch, the higher the mountain.

THE HIMALAYAS—OUR PLANET'S HIGHEST PEAKS!

I BET THERE WAS SOME SERIOUS QUAKING WHEN THEY WERE FORMED!

9

Tipping the Scales

When two plates bump against each other, they can cause some rocking and rolling in your town. How can you tell how bad the shaking was? Scientists measure earthquakes on the Moment **Magnitude** Scale, also known as the Richter Scale. The scale starts at 0 and goes up from there. Each number indicates a bigger, more violent earthquake. So, a magnitude 4 earthquake isn't as strong as a magnitude 5 or 6.

Most people don't notice an earthquake that is lower than magnitude 3.

Starting at magnitude 4, things can start to shake and fall.

At magnitude 5, weaker buildings may be damaged.

Beginning at magnitude 7, Earth's surface can crack open. Some buildings may collapse, and people can be killed by falling debris.

Monster quakes at 9 and above flatten cities. They happen about once every 5 to 10 years.

The **asteroid** strike that killed the dinosaurs 66 million years ago **may have set off earthquakes with a magnitude of about 13!**

Ripple Effects

All earthquakes have a lot of energy. A moderate magnitude 6 earthquake, for example, releases more energy than 6,000 tons (5,400 t) of dynamite! Earthquakes cause the ground to shift, cracks to open, trees to be uprooted, and rocks to roll. They also cause mudslides, landslides, and **avalanches**. Over millions of years, land changes caused by earthquakes push mountains upward, carve deep trenches, and redirect rivers.

In 2010, a huge quake moved the whole city of Concepción, Chile, about 10 ft (3 m) to the west.

An earthquake that struck China in the 16th century created cracks in the ground that were 60 feet (18 m) deep.

HEY! THIS RIVER DOESN'T BELONG HERE!

IT DOES NOW!

The earthquake in China caused huge floods and sparked fires that burned for days. It even lowered mountains and changed the paths of rivers.

A 1970 earthquake in Peru caused a landslide on Mt. Huascarán. It sent debris tumbling 100 miles per hour (160 kph) and killed tens of thousands of people.

Antarctica has icequakes. Water in the soil freezes, creating pressure that eventually explodes. This results in quake-like vibrations, tremors, and cracks.

A 2004 Indonesian quake was so powerful it moved the North Pole to the east by an inch (2.5 cm). It also made Earth spin faster by 2.68 microseconds.

The Ring of Fire

Earthquakes can often cause or be triggered by other natural disasters, such as mudslides, landslides, and flooding. And as if that isn't bad enough, earthquakes are also common around volcanoes, creating a potential for double disaster! So many volcanoes are found along the edges of the Pacific Ocean that the area earned the nickname the Ring of Fire. The 452 known volcanoes formed as the giant Pacific Plate ground into the other plates around it. These plate hot spots set off many earthquakes as well as volcanoes.

Sometimes, the flow of **magma** within a volcano **triggers earthquakes.**

About 75 percent of the world's volcanoes are found in the Ring of Fire. And 90 percent of all earthquakes happen there!

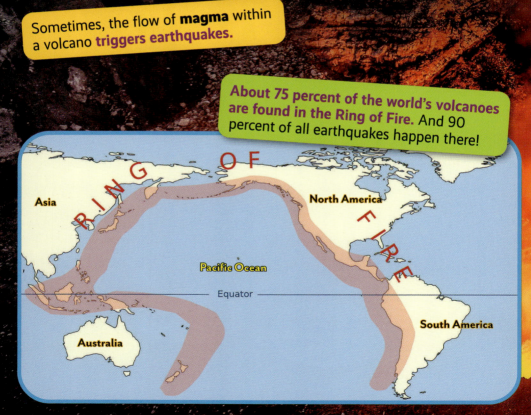

The Ring of Fire looks like a giant horseshoe. It is almost 25,000 miles (40,000 km) long.

The Pacific Plate moves northwest and the North American Plate slides southwest. They hit each other in California.

The huge San Andreas fault formed where the Pacific and North American plates collide. It is more than 800 miles (1,300 km) long.

Strong earthquakes happen along the San Andreas fault. After a 7.9 quake in 1906, fires nearly destroyed San Francisco, California.

In 1989, a magnitude 6.9 quake in San Francisco killed 63 people and made a major freeway bridge collapse.

WELL, IT WAS SAN ANDREAS'S FAULT.

WHAT A DISASTER! I WONDER WHAT CAUSED IT?

Cracking Up

There are many dangers that come from shaking beneath your feet. But when most people think of earthquakes, they often think of enormous cracks opening up in the ground. Earthquakes can cause **fissures** in the earth. Movies show these giant cracks caused by earthquakes swallowing people, cars, and entire towns, but in reality most fissures are too small and shallow to do that.

In rare cases, a fissure can be up to 2 miles (3 km) long and 90 ft (25 m) deep.

Research shows that most earthquake fissures open for only a brief time and then close up again.

Mongolia's 1957 quake opened a fissure that was deep enough to fit a full telephone pole inside it.

Walls of Water

Earthquakes don't just happen on dry land. They often strike under water, too. This type of quake is called a submarine or underwater earthquake. A 2011 quake that **devastated** Japan was centered about 80 miles (130 km) from shore! In the ocean, a quake's vibrations push huge amounts of water toward the shores, creating monster waves called tsunamis. These walls of water slam into coastal areas and do tremendous damage.

In Japanese, the word *tsunami* means harbor wave. **About 20 percent of the world's tsunamis form off the coast of Japan.**

The 2011 Japanese quake was magnitude 9. It triggered a tsunami with devastating waves.

The tsunami flooded Japan's Fukushima **nuclear** power plant, causing power failures, explosions, and the creation of dangerous waste.

18

In the Pacific Ocean, tsunamis can speed toward land at 430 miles per hour (690 kph).

Once they reach shallow coastal waters, tsunamis can rise up to be 100 ft (30 m) tall.

It usually takes a quake of at least magnitude 8 to generate a major tsunami.

On December 26, 2004, the world's most deadly tsunami swept across the Indian Ocean and thundered into surrounding coastlines, killing about 230,000 people.

I'M TALL!

I'LL SHOW YOU WHO'S TALL!

The tallest tsunami ever recorded roared into Alaska's Lituya Bay in 1958. It was 1,720 ft (520 m) tall, three times taller than Seattle's Space Needle.

A Monster Quake

Tsunamis, landslides, volcanoes, fissures—one monster earthquake had them all. On May 22, 1960, the earth started shaking violently in Chile. The magnitude 9.5 quake destroyed nearly half the city of Valdivia. Within 15 minutes, the underground tremors had stirred up a giant tsunami that towered 80 ft (25 m) high and barreled across the Pacific to Hawaii, Japan, and the Philippines. More than 6,000 miles (10,000 km) away from the initial shaking, 35-ft (10-m) waves nearly destroyed the Hawaiian city of Hilo.

THIS QUAKE WILL BE REMEMBERED FOREVER.

The Valdivia earthquake is the strongest one ever recorded.

The Valdivia quake's tsunami moved as fast as a jet plane and hit Hawaii 15 hours after the earthquake struck.

Foreshocks in and around Valdivia warned of the coming disaster. One was magnitude 8.1!

THE GROUND IS TREMBLING! IT IS TIME TO LEAVE THE CITY.

LET'S HURRY!

The foreshocks made many people flee the area early, probably saving thousands of lives.

Aftershocks shook Chile for a whole month! The quakes caused landslides so strong that they changed the flow of Chilean rivers.

Two days after the quake, a volcano that had been quiet for nearly 40 years erupted.

Death and Destruction

In addition to changing the landscape, earthquakes cause enormous destruction to human life and property. One of the deadliest natural disasters of all time occurred in China in 1556, when an earthquake of at least a magnitude 8.0 struck. The epicenter was in the Wei River valley, where millions of people lived in hillside cave dwellings. These homes collapsed during the quake, crushing the families within. Hundreds of thousands of people are thought to have died. And that was far from the only dangerous quake that left a mark.

In the wake of the 1556 quake, **Wei River valley residents rebuilt their homes with bamboo, wood, and other soft, more quake-resistant materials.**

A 1692 quake destroyed Port Royal, Jamaica, a town full of pirates from the Caribbean.

A deadly 7.0 magnitude earthquake in 2010 destroyed or severely damaged more than 280,000 buildings in Haiti.

In 2021, Haiti was still rebuilding from the 2010 earthquake when a 7.2 quake struck, killing more than 2,000 people and destroying more than 50,000 homes.

In 1964, a 9.2 magnitude quake destroyed downtown Anchorage, Alaska. Luckily, it was a holiday, so most buildings were empty.

Drop, Cover, and Hold!

When an earthquake causes things to fall off shelves and debris to rain down, you need to protect yourself. During an earthquake, you have to drop, cover, and hold. If you feel the ground start to shake, drop down on your hands and knees. This will stop you from falling over. Protect your head and neck by covering them with your arms and hands. If you can, seek additional cover under a sturdy desk or table and hold onto it. Then, stay where you are.

Every year, millions of people practice for quakes **on International ShakeOut Day.**

Stay away from windows and anything heavy or sharp that may fall on you!

I'M SCARED. LET'S RUN OUTSIDE!

STAY! WE'RE SAFER HERE!

There is a **myth** that you should run outside during a quake. But it's actually safer to take cover indoors.

Sometimes, teams of dogs are used to search for survivors.

Shaking but Not Breaking

There's no way to prevent earthquakes, but we can be prepared for them. **Engineers** have learned to make buildings, roads, and bridges stronger. We have learned how to fight against the powerful push-pull forces of a quake that can cause structures to collapse. To solve this, giant **pendulums** are now being hung in the upper floors of some skyscrapers. When a quake strikes and the building starts leaning in one direction, the pendulum swings the opposite way, steadying the structure. And that's just the beginning!

The ball of the giant pendulum swaying within the Taipei 101 skyscraper in Taiwan stands five stories tall.

Ancient buildings like the Parthenon in Greece have survived many earthquakes. By studying them, engineers get good ideas for designing quake-proof buildings!

IMPRESSIVE. AN EARTHQUAKE-PROOF BUILDING. WHAT'S YOUR SECRET?

METAL RODS.

One ancient trick that still works today is to **reinforce** buildings. Today, we use metal rods to keep buildings from falling down.

26

The Charilaos Trikoupis Bridge in Greece sits on posts driven deep into the ground. It sways like a hammock during a quake.

Spider silk is light but very strong! Scientists are creating lightweight quake-resistant building materials just like it.

Animals sometimes hide, cry, or panic before an earthquake. Scientists are trying to see if their odd behavior can help predict a coming quake.

Your cell phone may someday save your life! Just before a quake hit northern California in 2022, more than two million people received early warnings through their phones.

Fruity Fissures

Activity

Use an orange to learn about plate tectonics! Think of the orange as Earth and the peel as tectonic plates. Quakes happen where plates push together, and fissures form where those plates pull apart again.

Tectonic plates move slowly, grinding along at only 2 to 4 in. (5 to 10 cm) per year.

What You Will Need
- 1 orange
- A plastic knife
- A jar of jam

Earth's land was once all one supercontinent called Pangaea. Movements of tectonic plates caused Pangaea to split apart into the continents we have today.

Step One

Carefully peel an orange, keeping the skin in large pieces. You may need an adult to help.

Step Two

Tear the peel into four or five pieces. Each piece represents a tectonic plate.

Step Three

Put the peel back on the orange, lining up the pieces like a puzzle. What do you see where the edges meet?

Step Four

Take the pieces of peel off again and spread jam over the orange. The jam will act like the liquid rock that tectonic plates slide on.

Step Five

Put the pieces of peel back together on the orange. Notice how they slide more easily and can now overlap. Earthquakes happen when tectonic plates rub, overlap, and pull apart.

29

asteroid a small, rocky object that usually moves around the sun but ocassionally comes crashing into Earth

avalanches large amounts of snow, ice, earth, or rock that slide down a mountainside

debris broken pieces of something that has been destroyed

devastated ruined or destroyed

engineers designers or builders of engines and machines

eruptions explosions from volcanoes that let out lava, ash, steam, and gas

fissures openings or cracks along the ground

magma molten, or melted, rock within Earth

magnitude the size or extent of something

myth a popular or common belief that is not true

navigate to make one's way about, over, or through

nuclear relating to energy that is released when an atom is split

pendulums objects, such as balls or weights, hung from a fixed point that swing freely back and forth

reinforce to support and add strength

slabs thick, flat pieces of something

tectonic relating to Earth's crust

Read More

Dickman, Nancy. *Earthquake Disaster! San Francisco, 1906 (Doomed History)*. Minneapolis: Bearport Publishing, 2023.

McGregor, Harriet. *Flattened by an Earthquake! (Uncharted: Stories of Survival)*. Minneapolis: Bearport Publishing, 2021.

Van Rose, Susanna. *Volcano & Earthquake (DK Eyewitness)*. New York: DK Publishing, 2022.

Learn More Online

1. Go to **www.factsurfer.com** or scan the QR code below.

2. Enter **"X-treme Earthquakes"** into the search box.

3. Click on the cover of this book to see a list of websites.

Index

aftershock 7, 20

bridge 14, 26–27

buildings 4–5, 10–11, 23, 26–27

collapse 11, 15, 22, 26

core 8

crust 8–9, 17

debris 5, 11, 13, 24

epicenter 9, 22

faults 8–9, 15

fissure 16–17, 20, 28

floods 12, 14, 17–18

foreshock 6, 21

landslide 6, 12–14, 17, 20–21

mantle 8

mountains 9, 12

mudslide 12, 14

ocean 9, 14, 18–19

plates 8–10, 14–15, 28–29

pressure 6, 13

Richter Scale 10, 12

rivers 12, 21–22

surface 6, 8–9, 11

trench 9, 12

tsunamis 18–20

volcano 6, 14, 20–21

About the Author

Marcia Abramson lives in Ann Arbor, Michigan, a state that has few earthquakes.